A YOUNG BASEBALL PLAYER'S
GUIDE TO

FIELDING AND DEFENSE

ALSO BY DON OSTER

A Guide for Young Batters & Baserunners
with Bill McMillan

A Guide for Young Pitchers
with Bill McMillan

A Guide for Young Softball Pitchers
with Jacque Hunter

*A Young Softball Player's Guide
to Hitting, Bunting, and Baserunning*
with Jacque Hunter

All from The Lyons Press

A YOUNG BASEBALL PLAYER'S GUIDE TO

FIELDING AND DEFENSE

Don Oster and Bill McMillan

THE LYONS PRESS
GUILFORD, CONNECTICUT
An imprint of The Globe Pequot Press

The Lyons Press is an imprint of The Globe Pequot Press.

10 9 8 7 6 5 4 3 2 1

Printed in the United States of America

ISBN-13: 978-1-59228-847-2
ISBN-10: 1-59228-847-2

Library of Congress Cataloging-in-Publication Data

Oster, Don.
A young player's guide to fielding and defense / Don Oster and Bill McMillan.
p. cm. — (A young player's guide series)
ISBN 1-59228-847-2
1. Fielding (Baseball) 2. Baseball. I. McMillan, Bill, 1944- II. Title. III. Series.

GV870.O88 2006
796.357'25—dc22

2005028488

CONTENTS

ACKNOWLEDGMENTS

Bill and I want to again thank the hundreds of young players and coaches we worked with through the years. It is gratifying to note that now many of our former players are coaching baseball today at the youth level. We also must again thank our sons, Mike and Dave McMillan and Mark Oster. These boys were the reason we started coaching, and each of them handled the toughest job on any team (coach's son) very well.

We also must recognize Steve and Josh Santana, Tony and Matt Kremer, and Sean Godfrey who assisted with the photos. And thanks to the New Albany, Indiana, High School Athletic Department for allowing access to its field.

This is the third book in a series, which began with pitching for young players, followed by batting and baserunning, and concluding with this book on defensive play.

Our hope as authors is that young players reading these books will improve their skills, their understanding of the game, and have lots of fun playing this beautiful game.

—Don Oster

INTRODUCTION

Offense is obviously important to a team because you need to score runs to win ball games. A fundamentally sound offensive team can manufacture a couple of runs each game by getting some hits, bunting, advancing runners, and being aggressive on the bases. But it is really defense that wins games. A simple, sound defense will prevent an opponent from scoring and keep your team in every game. Of course, pitching is a big part of an effective defense, but pitchers certainly won't strike out all of the opponent's batters. How well the defense handles the plays on batted balls and base runners can determine the outcome of most ball games. Learning to play the defensive positions is what this book is all about.

The first three chapters introduce you to the basic skills needed to be a good position player. You will learn the fundamentals of fielding ground balls and fly balls, then making good throws. Included are techniques and practice drills in both text and photos. It is important to properly learn these skills at the start of your playing career. To develop the basic skills requires work and practice, practice, practice. The fundamentals and techniques of good fielding and throwing don't change as you grow older. The basics you learn now will apply as long as you play the game.

Next we cover position play. It isn't enough that you know how to field and throw well. Although these basics apply to all defensive positions, playing a specific spot well is much more complex. To be a good position player you must always know the game situation; it's called "having your head in the game." This means that you think ahead and know where to make a play when the opportunity arises.

As you begin your baseball career, it is important that you learn to play several positions. At a young age it is too early for you to try to specialize in any one position. Pitchers may also catch or play in the infield, outfielders may switch in and out of the infield, and so on. In short, the more positions you can play, the more valuable you are to your team, and the more likely you will be included in the lineup.

Each of the positions in a defense has several different jobs based on the game situation, which will be outlined as the position is covered. Some specific drills to practice for the positions are also described.

One final note. If you think defense isn't an important facet of the game, consider this: throughout the years professional baseball has had defensive specialists called "utility players." Many of these players could barely attain a batting average as high as their weight, yet they had long baseball careers based mainly on their ability to play several defensive positions well.

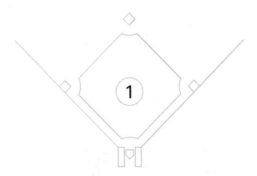

FIELDING GROUND BALLS

Most of this chapter deals with what you have to do to field ground balls well. It is about using proper techniques to field, but fielding is not just about techniques. Before the ball is hit, you should know what you will do with it when you get it. So think ahead.

THE BASICS

Fielding ground balls requires you to use your body in many different ways. However, three basics of fielding ground balls apply to most all situations.

The Ready Position

The ready position is the same for all fielders except the pitcher and catcher. It is important to be in the best position to move quickly in any direction before the pitcher throws the ball. Before the pitch, you should be comfortable and relaxed, and you should feel loose and flexible, not rigid or tense. Your feet should be shoulder width apart. You should be slightly bent forward at the waist, your knees should be slightly bent, and your eyes should be on the pitcher.

The ready position

As the pitching delivery begins toward the plate, your eyes move to focus on the batter. Never take your eyes off the ball until it is in your glove. At the same time, you should shift your weight to the balls of your feet. This weight shift will move your body slightly forward and cause your knees to bend, which will lower your body closer to the ground. You will want to be low when you field the ball, and the weight shift gets you ready to move to the ball. At the same time as you shift your weight, your hands move to an open position in front of you. Your hands should not be farther apart than the inside of your knees.

Glove Position

Many young players have problems with glove placement. The general rule to follow is that if the ball is above your waist, field it with the fingers of your glove pointing up. If the ball is to be fielded below your waist, the fingers of your glove should be pointed down. This same rule holds true for catching line drives or throws from other fielders.

A common problem with young players is that they try to trap or block the ball by having their fingers up when the ball is below their waist. It is also common to see young players raise their gloves above their waists with the fingers down. In either case, an error will likely occur. So remember this simple fingers up/fingers down rule.

Having your glove in the right position means that you can let the ball come to you. You don't have to reach for it from an awkward position. Once your glove is in the proper position, always use two hands to make the play. As the ball gets into your glove, make sure you secure the ball with your throwing hand. You will be able to make a quicker throw when you use two hands to catch the ball.

Glove placement is so important that you will want to spend a lot of time practicing it. You can practice with a friend who bounces balls above and below your waist. You can also practice this alone by throwing a rubber ball against a wall and fielding it.

Hands above the waist

Hands below the waist

If you hit the wall with a throw, the ball will usually come back at you below your waist. If you hit the ground first, the ball will usually skip off the wall and can be fielded above your waist.

Staying Low

As you move to the ball, stay low to the ground. Your first step to the ball is very important because if you raise up you will have to readjust your whole body to get down into a fielding position. It is easier to come up on a ball than it is to go down on one. Staying low gives you better balance when you field and puts you in a better position to throw.

GETTING GROUND BALLS

Regardless of the situation, there are four major things you must do to field ground balls well, and they are fundamental to everything else.

1. Get to the ball as fast as you can, but don't wildly attack the ball. Be smooth and under control as you move to the ball.
2. Play the ball, don't let the ball play you. Field the ball as you reach it; back up to field it only when it is absolutely necessary.
3. When you get to the ball, be in the best position to make a good throw. Maintain good body control and balance as you move to the ball. Catch the ball so that you are as close to a good throwing position as you can be.
4. Good footwork is the foundation to good fielding. When you watch good players field ground balls, you mostly focus on their hands and arms. However, your hands can't be in the

right position without good footwork. Your feet allow you to get into position to field the ball and make a good throw.

Balls Hit at You

Many ground balls in youth league games are balls that you can field directly in front of you. These are the routine plays. Some balls may be a little to your left or right, but you have time to get your body in front of the ball and use *the basic ground ball fielding position*. With practice, you should be able to make these plays almost every time.

The basic ground ball fielding position

When the ball is hit right at you, step forward with either foot. It doesn't matter which foot you use first, but be consistent. However, if the ball is hit a little to your right, your first step should be with your right foot. If the ball is hit a little to your left, your first step should be with your left foot. If the ball is slightly to your side, get in front of it by taking short sideways shuffle steps. To get to balls farther to either side will require using a crossover stride, as explained later.

As you move to the ball, stay low. When you get to the ball, your hands should be out in front of you and your knees should be bent. If you are right-handed, your left foot should be slightly in front of your right (plant) foot so that you are in a good position to throw. Lefties will have the right foot in front with the left foot as the plant foot. Let the ball roll into your glove, place your throwing hand on top of the ball, and smoothly bring your hands to your waist to start your throwing motion.

Starting the throwing motion

When you field the ball, try to have "soft hands," meaning they are not tense or rigid. Be relaxed, let the ball come to your glove. Don't lunge for or attack the ball with your hands. Fielders who attack the ball have "concrete hands." Let hard-hit balls come to you; move in on slower hits.

As you move into the fielding position, you have to be ready for the ball to take a bad hop. A bouncing ball may hit a pebble or clump of dirt and bounce high or dart to the right or left. This doesn't happen too often on good fields, but when it does, you have to be ready. The best way to be ready for a bad hop is to be in a good, basic fielding position with your hands in front of you and with your eyes fixed on the ball. Your hands should be loose and ready to move.

The throw from the ball hit at you is fairly easy because your feet are in position to throw when you field the ball. You simply take a short shuffle step with your plant foot, stride with your front foot, and throw the ball (usually overhand) right at your target. We recommend this " step, stride, and throw" technique for young players fielding routine ground balls at any position.

Infield Balls Hit to Your Right

Many times balls will not be hit so that you can get your body right in front of them. When the ball is hit far to your right, the technique used in getting to the ball is very different from the routine ball hit right at you. Your first move on balls hit to your right is to turn your right foot to the right. This movement will cause the rest of your body to start to turn to the right. The fastest way to get to the ball from this position is to use a "crossover step." This is done by crossing your left leg over and in front of your right leg. As you cross your left leg over, push with your right foot and take a long stride with your left leg. Now go get the ball. In many cases, you will probably have to "backhand" the ball, and you might be slightly off balance to throw. It is extremely important that you regain your balance to be in a solid position to throw. This is done by "planting" your right foot, squaring your shoulders to the target, and making a good, strong overhand throw. Good shortstops are often able to "go into the hole" behind third base and make this play look easy. A left-handed first baseman has this ball on his glove side, but he may need to take crossover steps to get to the ball. He has an easier play on these balls hit to his glove-hand (right) side.

Crossover step

Backhand catch

Infield Balls Hit to Your Left

When fielding ground balls hit to your left, your first move is to turn your left foot to the left and do the crossover step with your right leg. It is likely that your left arm will be fully extended when you reach the ball. In order to get yourself into a throwing position on this type of ground ball, you will have to fully turn your body so that your shoulders are square to the target. Depending on how far off the base he is playing, the left-handed first baseman may need to make the crossover step and a backhand catch to make a play on a ball hit near first base.

Crossover step

Field ball

Outfield Ground Balls

The techniques for fielding ground balls in the outfield are basically the same as they are for fielding ground balls in the infield. However, there is one major difference. When you get to the ball in the outfield, you usually have to throw it a lot farther than a ball fielded in the infield. This means that you should charge all ground balls that you can. Don't wait on the ball. Go after it hard, but stay on balance. If you jog after the ball, a fast runner can turn a single into a double or a double into a triple. When you get to the ball, square your shoulders and use the "step, stride, and throw" technique. Since your throw will be longer, take a longer stride and make a strong overhand throw to your target.

Sometimes young players are told to field outfield ground balls on one knee, which is supposed to help block the ball. Do not do this unless your coach absolutely insists on it. Fielding this way slows you down and gives all of the advantage to the offensive team.

PRACTICING

Any of the following four practice drills can be used at any time to help you learn or improve your fielding skills. Ideally, they can be used as a part of regular practice sessions. If not, you and your friends can do these drills before or after practice.

Verbal Positioning Drill

For this drill, you will need another person. One of you will be a fielder, and the other (the helper) will give verbal directions to the fielder. The fielder gets into the ready position, and the helper says either "at you," "right," or "left." Then the fielder should move properly, based upon the directions given, and make the fielding and throwing motions. One practice session should include about twenty directions.

Toss, Catch, and Throw Drill

Two people (a fielder and a tosser) are necessary for this drill. Once the fielder is in the ready position, the tosser should stand about twenty feet in front of the fielder and toss ground balls right at or to the right or left of the fielder. The fielder should use the proper techniques in fielding the ball and then throw it to the tosser. One practice session should include about twenty tosses, catches, and throws. Remember, the tossed ground balls and the return throws are meant to be thrown softly.

Pepper

To play pepper, a fielder and a hitter should be about twenty feet apart. The fielder gets into the ready position and tosses the ball underhand to the batter who punches the ball back to the fielder. This drill will result in balls going in many different directions. Remember, the fielder should toss the ball softly, and the hitter should take a very short swing. One practice session should include about forty hits and catches.

Live Fielding and Throwing

There is simply no substitute for practicing the techniques we have described in this chapter. The best way to develop the necessary skills for fielding ground balls is to field live ground balls off a bat. This will probably happen at most of your scheduled team practices. In addition, you and your friends should get together and make a game out of fielding. You might give three points for a good field and throw and two points for a good field but no throw. See how many grounders you can cleanly field in a row. Try to set a record. An endless number of games can be made out of fielding ground balls. Be creative and make it fun.

THINGS TO REMEMBER

1. Get to the ball as quickly as you can.
2. Develop good footwork.
3. Keep your eyes on the ball from the bat to the glove.
4. Play the ball. Don't let the ball play you.
5. When you field the ball, be in a good position to throw.
6. Have "soft hands."
7. Use the basic fielding position whenever possible.
8. There is no substitute for live practice.

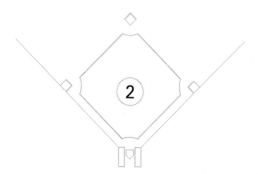

FIELDING FLY BALLS

Most of the fundamentals we discussed in chapter 1 are the same for fielding fly balls. Many fly balls in youth league games are hit to the outfield, and most of our examples will deal with techniques used by good outfielders.

As with fielding ground balls, you should start in the ready position discussed in chapter 1. This position allows you to move quickly in any direction. You need good footwork, and you need to get a good jump on the ball. You must get to the ball as fast as you can.

GETTING TO FLY BALLS

Effects of Wind, Sun, and Lights

When the ball is hit in the air, you should try to run to where you think the ball will go. In order to know where the ball is going, you have to pay special attention to the direction and strength of the wind. Also, for day games, you should know if the sun may be in your eyes as you move toward the ball. If it's a bright, sunny day, we recommend that you wear sunglasses or flip-ups. Old-time ball players used their gloves to keep the sun out of their eyes to field fly balls, and some players use an eye black grease under their eyes. Using sunglasses or flip-ups is far better.

For night games, you must pay attention to the height and glare of the lights. The most difficult play at night is when a fly ball is hit so that it seems to be above the height of the lights. This kind of ball will go from light to dark to light again, and it takes special concentration to make a catch on this kind of ball. If a ball is coming at you directly out of the lights, you will have to use your glove to shield your eyes from the glare. The important thing is to try to never take your eyes off the ball. During practices and especially during pregame warm-ups, pay special attention to the wind, sun, and lights. Doing these things will make you a better fielder.

A common term used in baseball is "high sky," which describes the sky on days when there are few or no clouds and a bright sun. Except for extremely windy days, the high sky is one of the hardest conditions for fielding fly balls. Without clouds it is difficult to tell how high a ball is hit. Practice judging fly balls when the sky is a high sky.

The Routine Fly Ball

For fly balls that are hit directly at you or slightly to your left or right, you should move to the ball and get into *the basic fly-ball fielding position.* Your left leg should be in front of your right leg, and your hands should be at shoulder height or above. The fingers of your glove should be pointing up, and your throwing hand should be ready to grasp the ball in the glove to complete the two-handed catch and start to throw. Do not rush or jump at the ball. Let it come to you.

The basic position for shielding eyes
from the sun with a bare hand

Balls Hit to Your Right or Left

The techniques for fielding fly balls to your right or left are basically the same as those used in fielding ground balls to your right or left. It is a good idea for you to review the parts of chapter 1 that deal with fielding ground balls. For the fly ball hit to the right, your first move is to turn your right foot out and use the crossover step with your left leg. Stay low during this move. Your strides will usually be longer than those of infielders because you will have more ground to cover. On plays to your left, your first move is to turn your left foot to the left and cross over with your right leg. When you make a catch in either direction, turn your shoulders to the target, set your plant foot, and do a "step, stride, and throw."

Ball hit to the left

Going In on the Ball

Many times a ball will be hit so far in front of you that you can't use the basic fly-ball fielding position. You must charge the ball. In order to stay on balance, you should keep low for your first two or three steps. It is easiest to make this play if you can catch the ball above your waist with the fingers of your glove pointed up. However, this play usually needs to be made below the waist. Try to catch the ball at knee level or above. We do not recommend that you try to make a "shoestring catch" when you are very young. It is better to catch the ball on one bounce, set yourself, and make a strong throw to the infield.

Going Back on the Ball

The basic techniques for going back on the ball are the same for infielders and outfielders. If the ball is hit over your right shoulder, turn your body to the right and look over your left shoulder when you are running. For balls hit over your left shoulder, turn to the left and look over your right shoulder. In either case, never take your eyes off the ball. A ball hit straight over your head is one of the most difficult plays in baseball. Your first step should be straight back, and you should turn in the direction the wind is blowing. For example, if you are a center fielder and the wind is blowing from your left to your right, you should turn to your right. When the ball is hit over your head in any direction, you should never, ever just keep backing up on the ball. You should always turn and move to the ball.

Line Drives Hit at You

Most experienced outfielders say that the most difficult ball to catch is the line drive that is hit directly at you. This catch is challenging because the ball can move and dart in the air, and it may be difficult to tell how hard the ball is hit. You should play this kind of ball differently than any other fly ball. On all other balls hit in the air, you should break as quickly as possible. On line drives hit at you, you should hesitate for a second. This hesitation will allow you to better judge the height and direction of the ball and will allow you to play the ball and not let the ball play you.

Running after Fly Balls and Pop-Ups

One of the most important things you can do is to run on the balls of your feet. If you run flat-footed, even if you have turned and have both eyes on the ball, the ball will look like it's moving in the air. The baseball can look like a Ping-Pong ball bouncing up and down. Running flat-footed will also slow you down. So always run to fly balls on the balls of your feet.

CATCHING AND THROWING

One of the most impressive plays in all of baseball is when an outfielder makes a catch or charges a ball and then guns the ball overhand on one bounce to throw out a runner. These kinds of plays can happen only if you are in the best position to throw when you catch the ball. You can't really separate a good throw from a good catching position.

Back—over the shoulder

Infield Pop-Ups

Fielding infield pop-ups is basically the same as catching fly balls in the outfield except that you will have to catch the infield pop-up more directly over your head. When the ball goes up, get to it as quickly as you can and call "mine" or "I've got it." It is important to know that pop-ups, especially those hit between the pitcher's mound and the backstop, will naturally move away from infielders and toward the backstop. This happens because of backspin on the ball. The best way to handle this situation is to move with the ball.

21

In order to make the best throws, you should try to be behind the ball when you catch it if at all possible. This means that you have reached the place where the ball is going and are waiting for it to come to you. A special technique to work on as you get older is to "run into the catch" when you need an especially strong throw. To do this, you need to be one or two strides behind where the ball is going to come down. You then catch the ball when you are moving forward. This technique will give you more power on the throw.

CATCHES NOT TO MAKE

As a young player, you should always remember that trying to make extraordinary or fancy catches can result in injury, help the other team, or both. We recommend that you do not try to make the following kinds of plays until you have had plenty of experience and practice.

1. Shoestring catches: trying to make impossible shoestring catches can turn a single into a double or worse.
2. Diving catches: if you must try a diving catch, do it with as much control as possible. Most injuries to outfielders are caused by diving after the ball. Knee and shoulder injuries are most frequent.
3. Basket catches: it is much more difficult to catch fly balls at your waist with the pocket of your glove facing up than to use the techniques we recommend. Willie Mays always used a basket catch. He did that because it came naturally to him and he was Willie Mays. Very few, if any, current major leaguers regularly use the basket catch. You shouldn't either.

4. One-handed catches: you will make more catches and make quicker throws if you catch the ball with two hands rather than with one.

5. Catches against the wall: most young players want to run to the wall, jump high, and save a home run. However, make sure that you don't run into the wall at full speed and hurt yourself. Use good judgment.

PRACTICING

Fielding fly balls requires a great deal of judgment, and the best way to develop good judgment is to practice a lot. The following drills are similar to those we recommend for fielding ground balls.

Verbal Fly-Ball Drill

Two people are required for this drill, a fielder and a helper. The fielder should get into the ready position, and the helper should say either "at you," "right," "left," "in" or "back." The fielder should go through the complete fielding and throwing motions for each command. This drill should be done about twenty times per session.

Fly-Ball Toss, Catch, and Throw Drill

Two people are required for this drill, a fielder and a tosser who should be about twenty feet apart. The tosser softly tosses a fly ball right at, to the right and left, or in front of or behind the fielder. The fielder should catch the ball and throw it back to the tosser. This drill should be done about twenty times per session.

Live Fielding and Throwing

Most practices include this kind of activity, which is the best way to learn how to field fly balls. Additional practice with your friends will be necessary for you to become a really good fielder of fly balls. Catch and throw as many fly balls as you can using the techniques in this chapter.

THINGS TO REMEMBER

1. Be aware of the wind, sun, and lights.
2. Use the basic fly-ball fielding position as often as possible.
3. When you catch the ball, try to be in the best position to throw.
4. Always run on the balls of your feet.
5. Fully set yourself and square your shoulders before you throw from the outfield.
6. Play it safe. Save the fancy catches until you get older.
7. Practice.

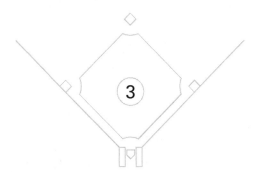

MAKING ACCURATE THROWS

People have been throwing balls of one kind or another for centuries, which is a natural thing to do. However, to make strong and accurate baseball throws, there are some basic things that you will have to learn. Different kinds of throws are used in baseball, and throwing involves using your whole body, not just your arm.

THE MECHANICS OF THROWING

The way you use your body to throw a baseball is called the mechanics of throwing. We emphasize the mechanics of the overhand throw because it is by far the most common throw used in youth league games. Please note that when we refer to an "overhand" throw, we are talking about both the three-quarter (halfway between straight overhand and sidearm) and the straight overhand motions.

Throwing a baseball is a highly coordinated act. Study the throwing sequence below so that you can see the throwing motion from beginning to end. Each important part of throwing mechanics is discussed separately so that we can point out how to do each one most effectively.

Square to target

Stride and lay back

Release

Follow through

The Grip

When you reach into your glove to grab the ball with your throwing hand, try to get the same grip on the ball every time. A consistent grip will help you make accurate throws. Because your hands are probably still pretty small compared to the size of the ball, we recommend that you grip the ball with your index and middle fingers where the seams are closest together. You should grip the ball either "with" or "across" the seams.

If you grip the ball with the seams, the seams should point away from you and your index and middle fingers should rest comfortably on top of the seams. For the grip across the seams, your index and middle fingers lie across the seams. The closer to the tips of your fingers that you can hold the ball, the harder you will be

28

able to throw it. With either grip, your index and middle fingers should be spread with your thumb on the bottom of the ball, directly under your index finger. Your third finger should rest on the side of the ball. Try both grips to see which one works best for you.

With the seams, two-fingered grip

Across the seams, two-fingered grip

Squaring Up to the Target

No matter where you field the ball, square your shoulders to the target. As you are squaring your shoulders, you move your feet into a throwing position, and your hands come in to your body.

The Stride

As your arm starts to move backward, your weight shifts to your plant foot. You now push off with your plant foot and stride with your other (front) leg. As your front foot hits the ground, your front shoulder begins to open up, and your throwing arm and shoulder start forward.

You should always take a comfortable stride and be sure to land on the ball of your front foot. Don't think about overstriding or understriding. What is comfortable to you is the stride you naturally want to use.

The stride shifts your weight from your back foot to your front foot. You actually throw off your front foot. Always remember that you stride to throw.

The Layback

As you begin to stride, your glove hand moves forward and your throwing hand moves back. The farther back you can extend your arm, the harder and farther you will be able to throw. If you need to make a short, quick throw, you can bring the ball just behind your head and make a "snap throw." A long or powerful throw requires full extension.

Arm and Wrist Motion

As your arm comes forward, your right elbow comes through first. Your upper arm (from the elbow to the shoulder) is parallel to the ground. Your wrist should be in a "cocked" position. This is important because as your arm comes forward, the last part of the throw requires a snap of your wrist. You should snap your hand forward in a smooth, quick motion and pull down on the ball with your fingers.

Release Point

If you have good mechanics up to this point, the accuracy of your throws will be controlled by your release point. The release point is where you let the ball go in front of you. If you let the ball go too soon, you will throw high. Hold it too long and you will throw it low. As a young player, your release point may vary from time to time. It is especially important to establish your release point during pregame warm-ups.

The Follow-Through

After you release the ball, your throwing arm should continue in a smooth arc toward the ground. Your right leg should swing around, and you should finish the throw with your chest facing the target.

INFIELD AND OUTFIELD THROWS

Throws made by infielders and outfielders can be quite different. An infielder must be especially quick in getting rid of the ball.

The layback for infield throws seldom, if ever, reaches full extension, but the layback for an outfielder's throw usually reaches full extension. The release point is higher for outfielders because of the greater distance the ball needs to travel.

At times, infielders can make a snap throw from right behind the head, but outfielders do not make snap throws. Infielders should always try to aim the ball between the chest and the belt buckle of the player they are throwing to. On balls hit deep to the outfield, the shortstop or second baseman will come into the outfield to make a relay throw to the infield, which is also called a cutoff play. Outfielders should try to make the cutoff throw to the infielder chest high.

When trying to throw out runners on short throws, throw the ball about knee high right over the base. For longer throws when you can't reach the base, throw the ball on one hop to the infielder or catcher covering the base. A throw over the base allows the infielder or catcher to get into the best position to catch the ball and make the tag.

OTHER KINDS OF THROWS

Sometimes an infielder does not have time to make an overhand throw, but there are two other ways for the throw to be made—underhand and sidearm. The underhand throw is used on a slowly hit ground ball that the infielder must charge, field, and throw, basically in one motion. Players will usually field this kind of ball with their throwing hand.

The sidearm throw is used when the infielder needs to make a longer throw and does not have time to square and throw overhand.

It is also used for short, quick infield throws. Many major league infielders make good use of sidearm throws, especially when they are throwing to a base other than first base.

The underhand and sidearm throws are discussed here for you to practice as you grow and develop physically. Because it is very hard for young players to be accurate with either of these throws, we strongly recommend that you first master a good overhand throw as the foundation of your throwing game.

PRACTICING

Throwing is so much a part of baseball that you will have a lot of chances to practice the fundamentals in team practices or when playing baseball with your friends. Three things are especially important to keep in mind when practicing throwing.

1. Take care of your arm: always stretch your arm and warm up slowly for about ten or fifteen minutes before you start to throw hard. Start playing catch at thirty feet and throw for at least five minutes from sixty feet. If your arm is sore or injured, there is no place in the field that you can play.

2. Always practice good fundamentals: we have seldom seen a practice or game that doesn't start with playing catch, but too often, these warm-ups look more like chaos than practice. Prepractice and pregame warm-ups are a very convenient time to practice throwing. Always make accurate throws, and try to hit your teammate in the chest with every throw. Concentrate on squaring your shoulders and using good fundamentals to hit your target.

3. Practice a quick release: in order to get fast runners out, infielders should practice quick footwork and hand movement. A good way for you to improve your skills is to pair up with a teammate, stand about forty-five feet apart, and see how many catches and throws can be made in a minute.

THINGS TO REMEMBER

1. Good mechanics result in accurate throws.
2. Throws made by infielders and outfielders are quite different.
3. Master a good overhand throw and use it before you try sidearm or underhand throws.
4. Use pregame and prepractice warm-up sessions to practice your throwing fundamentals.
5. Take good care of your arm.

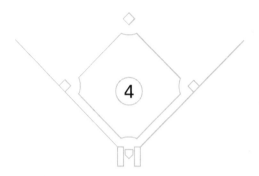

PLAYING THE
OUTFIELD POSITIONS

In the first three chapters of this book, we discussed the fundamentals of fielding and throwing. In this chapter, we deal with the responsibilities and strategies of outfield play.

CHARACTERISTICS OF OUTFIELDERS

Although each outfield position requires somewhat different skills, all outfielders must act as a coordinated unit in order to provide good defensive play.

The Center Fielder

Center field is the most important of the outfield positions. The center fielder is the captain of the outfield, and the players who play this position are expected to take charge of all balls hit to the outfield. Center fielders should field all balls they can get to, within reason. If the center fielder calls out, "mine" or "I've got it," the right fielder or left fielder is expected to let the center fielder make the play.

Because center fielders have to cover more ground and make more plays than other outfielders, they are usually the best athletes in the outfield. They usually run faster and, on youth teams, often have better arms than the other outfielders. They also have to have good judgment, so that they will know when to play the ball or let someone else make the play.

The Left Fielder

Left field is an important position on youth league teams because most young players bat right-handed and hit the ball to the left side of the infield and outfield. Left fielders don't have to be fast and can do quite well with only average speed.

Left fielders make the shortest throws of all outfielders and don't need great arms. What they need most is the ability to consistently catch the ball cleanly and make accurate throws.

The Right Fielder

On youth league teams, right field is the least important of the outfield positions. This is because there are fewer left-handed than right-handed batters and fewer balls are hit to the right side. The right fielder should be able to make routine plays and accurate throws.

POSITIONING

Knowing where to play hitters is a key part of outfield defense. Good positioning simply helps you get to the ball as soon as possible. Most outfield positioning will be directed by your coach, who may want you to play straightaway, in, back, or to your left or right. However, there are still some things that you need to think about. Remember, outfielders are a coordinated unit.

Playing Straightaway

When you play straightaway, which is the basic outfield position, you are in the middle of your position. This means that the distance between the center fielder and the left fielder is the same as the distance between the center fielder and the right fielder. The center fielder is directly behind second base.

Shifting to the Left or Right

When you shift toward left field or right field, you should keep the same distance between the outfielders as you had in the straightaway position. If a right-handed pull hitter is at bat, the outfield shifts toward the left field foul line. The right fielder should take two or three steps toward the infield. This is good positioning because most opposite-field hits in youth league games tend to be hit off the end of the bat and don't carry very far. In situations where the outfield shifts toward the right field foul line, the left fielder should take two or three steps forward.

Playing Deep or Shallow

For power hitters, outfielders almost always shift deep and to the hitter's power field (left field for right-handed hitters and right field for left-handed hitters). For weak hitters, the outfielders usually play more shallow and straightaway.

Knowing the Other Team

Always keep track of where the hitting team is in its batting order. Is this hitter just trying to get on base? Is this the cleanup hitter? It makes a difference, and it may even be helpful to think about the batting order of your own team.

The top of the batting order (number one, number two, and number three) includes good hitters who make good contact and can handle the bat. Number three hitters will be the best overall hitters on the team because they will hit the ball hard and they usually have power. You will want to play the number one and number two hitters straightaway and number three hitters shifted toward the hitter's power field. The hitters in the top of the order usually have good speed. Don't let them take the extra base on you.

The middle of the batting order (number four, number five, and number six) makes up the power of the lineup. The number four (cleanup) hitter will have the most power on the team. For cleanup hitters, you should shift toward the hitter's power field and move back two or three steps. The number five and number six hitters require less of a shift, but you will still need to respect these hitters.

The bottom of the batting order (number seven, number eight, and number nine) includes the weakest hitters on the team. You should play shallower for these hitters, as they will usually swing late on pitches and hit the ball to the opposite field. Therefore, the outfielders may want to take a step or two in the opposite direction from the hitter's power field. That is, for a right-handed hitter, the outfielders would shift toward the right field foul line.

Knowing Your Pitcher

Where the ball is hit has a lot to do with where and how hard the pitcher is throwing the ball. High pitches are usually hit in the air; low pitches are usually hit on the ground. Although good hitters will be able to pull the ball on slow pitchers, they may not be able to get around on very fast pitchers. See if the hitter is swinging early, late, or has the pitcher timed. Also, if a pitch is on the outside part of the plate, hitters will not be able to pull the ball as easily as when the ball is from the middle of the plate in. Good outfielders are often said to be "moving at the crack of the bat," which means that one of the main things these players do is to let pitcher speed and location tell them where the ball is most likely to be hit.

Calling Fly Balls

In general, center fielders should catch everything they can get to. *However, the outfielder who calls for the ball first should catch the ball.* If the right fielder calls "I've got it" or "mine" first, then the center fielder should slow down and let the right fielder make the play. If the center fielder and another outfielder call for the ball at the same time, the center fielder should continue to call for the ball and make the play. Avoid outfield collisions, and remember, "I've got it . . . no, you take it" is not a good call.

BACKING UP PLAYS

Outfielders are the last line of defense, so each outfielder has a responsibility for backing up infielders and other outfielders.

Backing Up the Infield

If the ball is either hit or thrown in your direction, you should move in to back up the play. For example, the right fielder backs up all ground balls hit to the right side of the infield, all balls thrown to first base, and throws to second from either third base or shortstop. The center fielder backs up all balls in the middle of the infield. The left fielder covers all balls hit or thrown to the left side of the infield. As with all other parts of outfield play, center fielders back up all balls they can get to in right center or left center field.

Backing Up Outfielders

If a ball is hit to the outfield, another outfielder should always back up the outfielder who is making the play. If a ball is hit to right center and the center fielder takes the ball, the right fielder should back up the play. If the right fielder makes the play, the center fielder should be the backup. The left fielder and center fielder have the same responsibilities for balls hit into left center.

The center fielder backs up balls hit directly at either the left fielder or right fielder. On balls hit right at the center fielder (especially slowly hit ground balls) both of the outfielders should be moving to be backups.

THE SHORT FLY BALL

A common play in youth league games, and one of the most dangerous, is the short fly ball between an infielder and an outfielder. The infielder turns and is going back on the ball, while you, the outfielder, are charging in on the ball. Your eyes and your teammate's eyes are focused on the ball.

As the outfielder, you should take charge of the play because it is much easier to go in on a ball than to go back. As soon as you can, make the call "I've got it" or "mine." The infielder should go after the ball until you call him off, and if you are sure you can make the catch, make the call quickly and loudly.

HITTING THE CUTOFF

Knowing where to throw the ball when you get it in the outfield is one of the most complicated parts of baseball. Even major leaguers make serious mistakes in "throwing to the wrong base." When you watch major league games, the expert analyst will point these out.

One of the worst youth league plays to see is an outfielder picking up the ball, holding it, looking around, and holding it some more as runners circle the bases. This should never happen. We have had good success in coaching youth league teams by using the following method that makes the throws from the outfield as simple as possible.

In youth league baseball, the major throwing responsibility of the outfielders is to throw to the player who is taking the cutoff. Depending upon where the ball is hit, the cutoff is taken by either the second baseman or the shortstop, and your job is to get the ball to the cutoff as soon as possible.

On balls hit to the right of second base (i.e., right field or right center) the second baseman is the cutoff. On all other balls, the shortstop (who is probably one of the best athletes on the team) should take the throw and complete the play.

Given this kind of cutoff method, you only have to remember to square your shoulders and make a strong and accurate throw that hits the cutoff in the middle of the chest. Remember, always hit the cutoff in the chest.

PLAYING FIRST BASE

First base is a very busy place. Fielders throw the ball there and hitters want to get there. Besides the pitcher and catcher, the person who plays first base handles the ball more often than anyone else on the field, which means that the first baseman needs to be a good athlete.

CHARACTERISTICS OF A GOOD FIRST BASEMAN

A good first baseman is usually taller than average because a larger target is easier for other infielders to throw to. Also, playing first base requires a good deal of stretching for throws, and a tall player can reach balls that shorter players can't reach. A good first baseman must be flexible and have good hands and good footwork.

First base is the only defensive position that gives a clear advantage to left-handed throwers who are at a disadvantage at all other infield positions. The left-handed first baseman is in a better position to throw the ball to second or third than a right-handed thrower. Because their glove is on their right hand, lefties can cover more ground in the hole between first and second. However, it is very possible for a right-handed thrower to be a great first baseman, and many outstanding right-handed first basemen have made baseball history.

POSITIONING

Because a great majority of youth leagues (for players twelve years old and younger) do not allow runners to lead off the bases, positioning for the first baseman is very simple. When signaled by the coach, the first baseman plays in on sacrifice bunt situations, and in other situations the coach may want the whole infield or just the first baseman or third baseman in. Otherwise, where the first baseman plays is totally dependent on the hitter. Hitters who might bunt for a hit should be played a step or two in front of the base. Left-handed pull hitters and power hitters need to be played deep and toward the line. Right-handed power or pull hitters need to be played two or three steps to the right. All other players should be played ten or fifteen feet from the first baseline and one step behind the base.

CATCHING THE BALL

The first and most important responsibility of the first baseman is to catch the ball. Leave the base if you have to, but catch the ball.

If a throw gets past you, a ball hit ten feet in front of the plate might turn into a costly error.

Position to receive a good throw

Receiving the Throw

When the ball is hit to an infielder, you should move to the position that gives you the ability to go quickly in any direction. Turn your body to face the direction of the throw. Your feet should be about six inches in front of the base and about shoulder width apart. Your knees should be slightly bent, and you should bend slightly forward at the waist. Both hands should be chest high in front of you to make a target for the throw. This gets you into a solid, balanced position to start the play. As the ball is fielded, move your foot back to feel the base to begin moving into a receiving position. In the receiving position left-handers should place their left foot on the base and stride with their right leg. Right-handers should place their right foot on the base and stride with their left leg. When the ball is thrown, keep your foot on the base and stride toward the throw to make the play.

Routine Plays

Many times, a fielder will field the ball cleanly and make a strong, chest-high throw. On those kinds of plays, simply place the proper foot on the front of the bag, take a short, comfortable stride, and make the catch. On every play at first, get your foot off the base as soon as possible to avoid being stepped on.

Throws to Your Right or Left

On throws to your right or left, you want to be in a position to stretch as far as you can. On throws to the right, left-handers do a straight stride with their right leg. Right-handers should keep their right foot on the base and do a crossover stride with their left leg. On a throw to the left, the right-hander takes a straight stride, and the left-hander uses a crossover stride.

High Throws

One of the most common mistakes that young players make is to try to keep their foot on the base while they reach for a ball that is too high to catch without jumping. Remember, the main job of the first baseman is to catch the ball. It is better to jump for the ball and then touch the base than for the ball to hit the top of your glove and roll away. Ideally, when you have to jump for the ball, try to do it so that you land on top of the base. This move will save you the time you would lose in trying to locate and touch the base.

Throw to the right

Throw to the left

Throws in the Dirt

Fielding balls in the dirt is probably the most difficult play for the first baseman. Good judgment is the key to making these plays well.

Catching the ball on a big hop is the easiest play you can make. However, most of the time the ball will take a low hop out in front of you or at your feet. If you can make a long stretch and catch the ball in front of you before it hops, that is your best choice on balls thrown low. If you don't think you can reach the ball, your next best choice is to stay back by the base and hope you will get a good hop. The most impressive of your choices is to scoop the ball after either a short or long stride. To scoop the ball, you move the glove underhand and forward in one motion and catch the ball on a short hop. This play is the riskiest of the choices, but a good first baseman can usually make it.

Scoop a low throw

If you are serious about playing first base, you will need to practice these plays. Drills to practice catching throws in the dirt are usually a part of regular team practices, especially early in the season. Infield practice, which is a part of almost all team practices, is another good place to learn. It is always a good idea to pair up with a friend who throws balls in the dirt to you. Remember, you should practice enough so that making these plays becomes automatic.

Wide Throws

On balls that are thrown too far to your right or left for you to reach by stretching, you will have to leave the base to catch the ball. As with high throws, your first job is to catch the ball. If you can't get back to the base before the runner gets there, your best choice is to try to tag the runner with the ball held firmly in your glove with both hands. You see this play most often when the ball is thrown wide and toward home plate. A good first baseman will simply catch the ball, wait for the runner near the first baseline, and apply the tag.

Throws from the Catcher

On balls that are just tapped and fielded by the catcher in front of the plate, the base runner may be in the way of the throw from the catcher to the first baseman. On this play, the first baseman's receiving position needs to be adjusted. Place your left foot on the inside of the base with your feet spread wide to make a big target inside the baseline. You should be fully facing the catcher and have a chest-high target. This position allows the catcher to make a throw that will not hit the runner.

Position to receive a throw on a bunt near the line

Sometimes a very weakly hit or bunted ball will be right on the first baseline. On this play, it is best for you to get into a receiving position that allows the catcher to throw the ball to you in foul territory. To do this, you place your right foot on the foul ball side of the base with your feet spread wide to make a big target outside the baseline. Once again, your target should be about chest high.

FIELDING PLAYS

A good first baseman needs to make many different kinds of fielding plays. Only the major fielding plays that happen most often in youth league games are discussed below.

The Unassisted Putout

When you can field the ball and beat the runner to the base with no help, this is called an unassisted putout. Step on the side of the base and get out of the way of the runner. On balls hit to you, the pitcher should be coming over to help. To make the unassisted putout, stop the pitcher by holding your hand up and calling "I've got it" or "mine."

Position to receive a ball from the catcher in foul territory

The Pitcher Covering the Base

On balls hit a step or two to your right or well behind the base, you will probably not be able to beat the runner to the base. In this case, the pitcher should be covering first base. When you field the ball, show it to the pitcher at all times. We recommend that young players make a soft, overhand throw to the infield side of the base in order to protect the pitcher from a collision with the runner.

Sacrifice Bunts

Your coach will tell the team how to defend bunts. If you are expected to field a bunt, play two or three steps in front of the base and charge when the batter squares to bunt. If the pitcher covers the first baseline, you simply stay in your regular position.

When you field a bunt, the catcher or some other designated player will tell you which base to throw to. Do not hesitate. The second baseman will cover first base. On throws to second base, be careful not to hit the runner going to second. On the throw to third base, you will have to make a hard throw because of the distance. No matter where you are told to throw a bunted ball, you will need to make a quick pivot to square your shoulders to the target and make a quick, accurate throw.

The Force-Out at Second Base

When a first baseman fields a ball with a runner on first base and fewer than two outs, there is always a choice to make. Do you throw to second base or get the out at first? In almost all cases, we recommend you take the out at first if it is a routine play, especially if you can get an unassisted putout. The only exception is if a ball is fielded far to your right and you can keep a runner out of scoring position by making the play at second base.

Cutoff Plays

Another type of cutoff play occurs when a runner is in scoring position, a ball is hit to the outfield, and there will be a throw to the plate. Most coaches use the first baseman as a cutoff for throws to home plate. The simple principle for cutoffs is that you position yourself at about forty or forty-five feet from home plate and form a straight line between the thrower and the catcher. The ball should be thrown at your chest, and if the catcher says, "cut one, cut two, or cut three," catch the ball and throw it to the base indicated (e.g., "cut two" means to throw to second base). If the catcher says "let it go" or "no," step aside and let the throw go through.

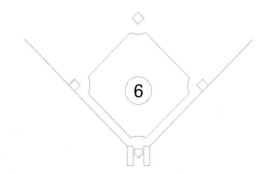

PLAYING SECOND BASE

The second baseman and shortstop make up the middle infield part of a strong defense "up the middle." Second base is a key position that on the surface may look simple. However, the second baseman must handle several responsibilities beyond fielding ground balls and throwing out runners. Many of the second baseman's jobs require communication and coordination with the shortstop, and several plays require the second baseman and shortstop to act as a team.

CHARACTERISTICS OF A GOOD SECOND BASEMAN

A second baseman should have quick feet. He must be able to quickly cover a lot of ground to field ground balls. He doesn't need to have the strongest throwing arm in the infield to throw out runners because he is close to both first base and second base. But quick hands and a quick release when making throws are important. The second baseman must be fundamentally sound when fielding ground balls, employ good footwork, and be balanced when making throws.

POSITIONING

The normal straightaway position for the second baseman is between first and second base, about two-thirds of the way to second, and about six steps back of the baseline. You would be in this back position for most batters in the lineup when there are no outs and no runners on base. This back position gives you more time to get to balls hit to either side and to cut off base hits. And you have more time to throw out the runner because you are the closest infielder to first base.

You should make adjustments based on certain circumstances that will give you a jump on where balls are likely to be hit. If your pitcher is very fast, expect most of the batters to have a late bat. Move two or three steps toward first base for right-handed batters and two or three steps toward second base for lefties. If your pitcher throws with normal speed, stay in the regular position until you see a reason to move. Watch batters' swings and foul balls. Shift toward first for a lefty who tends to pull the ball toward the right field line or a right-handed batter who tends to hit the ball to the opposite field. Shift toward second base for a right-handed batter who tends to pull the ball or a lefty who tends to hit to the opposite field.

Double Play Depth

With fewer than two outs and a runner on first base, you should move in toward the plate two or three steps. This gives you a better opportunity to execute the double play with the shortstop. In youth baseball, short-to-second-to-first double plays aren't executed very often, but in this situation you are expected to at least get the lead runner out.

Playing In

In a close game in the late innings with a runner on third base, your coach will likely tell the infield to pull in to get the runner trying to score. You should move in to a position at or just inside the baseline. If the bases are loaded, the play is a force at home and your play will always be to the plate. If the bases aren't loaded, look back at the runner on third. If the runner on third tries to score, throw him out at the plate. If he doesn't break toward the plate, throw out the runner going toward first base.

Pop-Ups and Fly Balls

You will call "I've got it" and catch fly balls or pop-ups in your area unless the ball is near first base and the first baseman calls for the ball. You go out after fair and foul balls hit to short right field and on the right field side of center field. The right or center fielder has the better chance to make these plays because either player is coming in to make the catch. Because you are moving out into the outfield, an over-the-shoulder catch is one of the most difficult plays for you to make. If you can get into position to make the catch, call for it, but be ready for an outfielder to call you off.

Covering Bases

When a runner is on first, anticipate an attempted steal on each pitch. After the pitch passes the batter, break toward second base to get a head start on a runner. For runners trying to steal second, conventional baseball wisdom has the second baseman covering second base when there is a right-handed batter, with the short-stop covering when a lefty is at the plate. An exception to this is when you are shifted toward first for a late-swinging right-handed batter or your pitcher is extremely fast and you are shaded toward second for a left-handed batter. Always talk to your shortstop and reach agreement on who will cover the base on an attempted steal.

You will cover first base when the first baseman goes after a fly ball or pop-up. You also must cover first base on a bunt defense if the first baseman charges toward the plate. When the first baseman plays a slow roller, you go to cover first base. But, if the pitcher is moving up the line to make the play, pull out to back up the throw.

The second baseman covers second base on balls hit to the left or straightaway center field. (The shortstop will go into the field to line up in position to take a relay throw.)

Relay and Cut off Plays

On balls hit to the outfield to the right side of second base, the second baseman goes into the field to set up as a cutoff man or to make a relay throw. In all cases, face the outfielder making the play and raise your arms to give him a target for a throw. When the batter hits a single and there are no runners on base, take a position between the fielder and second base. The shortstop will tell you whether to let the throw through or cut it off, and either hold the ball or throw to the base. If you cut off any relay and the runners hold, *always run the ball back to the infield.*

When there is an extra-base hit to the right side, or a hit to right field with runners on base, go into the outfield to make a relay throw. Move to a position about ninety to one hundred feet from the outfielder. Align yourself between the outfielder and a point halfway between third base and home plate. Take the throw from the outfielder with your body slightly turned to the left. (This makes it quicker for you to turn, step, and make a throw.) The shortstop should tell you to either hold up or throw to a base.

Backing Up Plays

When there are no runners on base, back up all throws to first base from the third baseman, shortstop, pitcher, and catcher. Also back up plays at second base when the shortstop is covering the base. If you are to cover second, back up the pitcher on all return throws from the catcher.

Making Tags

Sprint to the bag to cover second. Position your feet on either side of the base and face the player making the throw. Be alert for a bad throw. Focus first on catching the ball. If the throw is off target, go after it, catch it, then apply the tag. To apply the tag, grasp the ball with your bare hand inside the pocket of your glove. This will keep the runner from knocking the ball out of your hands.

Keep tags low in front of base

Bend down and hold the glove in front of the first base side of the base where the runner will slide into the tag. Be sure to hold the glove low. Many runners can slide under a high tag.

The Double Play

With a runner on first or runners on first and second with fewer than two outs, pull in two or three steps from your normal position to double play depth. The play is on when a ground ball is hit toward your position. Take things in order. First, make sure you field the ball. Pivot on your right foot, step toward second base, and toss the ball to the shortstop covering the bag. If you field the ball close to the bag you may lob the ball underhanded. The farther from second base you field the ball, the harder you must make the toss. Make the ball easy for the shortstop to handle by aiming at his chest. At a minimum you want to make sure to force the lead runner. The shortstop will try to complete the double play by throwing to first.

When the grounder is to the shortstop, sprint to second base. Be ready for a bad throw. If the throw is right at you, step over the bag with your right foot as you receive the throw. Tag the bag by dragging your left foot across it, then step toward first base with your left foot to throw out the runner. If the throw is to your left, catch the ball, tag the bag with your right foot as you plant it, and step toward first with your left foot to make the throw. To handle a

Tag base – set – throw

throw to your right, step out with your right foot to catch the ball. Drag your left foot across the base to make the tag, then step your left foot toward first to make the throw.

If you field the ball near the base, call off the shortstop and take the play yourself. Go to the bag, step on it for the force, and relay to first. If the ball is a hard grounder, it is almost a certain twin kill. Use whatever footwork is comfortable and concentrate on making a good throw.

When you field a ground ball near the baseline, glance at the runner advancing toward second base. If the ball is hit hard, you may be able to tag the runner to start the double play. Tag him with your glove, holding the ball in your bare hand in the pocket of your glove. If he runs three feet out of the baseline to avoid the tag, he should be called out. If the grounder is a slow roller, you may not have time to get the force at second. When the play looks too close, go for the out at first. This is a judgment call, but you don't ever go too far wrong by getting a runner out.

The footwork to make the force at second and a good relay throw to first takes practice to master. This is difficult because when you go to take the throw to tag the bag, your momentum is away from first base. Practice the double play routine with your shortstop until it becomes automatic.

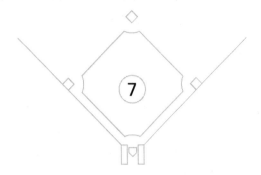

PLAYING SHORTSTOP

Coaches normally select one of the best athletes on the team to play shortstop, and it is common on many teams to see a shortstop who is also one of the better pitchers. The shortstop must have quick feet and the speed to cover a lot of ground when fielding balls hit into the hole toward third base or up the middle toward second base. The shortstop doesn't have a lot of time to make plays, so he also must have quick hands, a quick release on throws, and a strong arm. Good balance and footwork are necessary to make the needed, accurate throws to retire runners.

A good defense is structured to be "strong up the middle." The shortstop makes up part of the core of this defense, which includes the pitcher, catcher, second baseman, and center fielder.

Many teams designate the shortstop as team captain. He or the catcher may be the "holler guy" or team leader on defense. Being always aware of the game situation, he reminds the other fielders of the number of outs and where plays are to be made.

POSITIONING

The shortstop's normal straightaway position is about one-third of the way between second and third bases. Most of the plays will be to field the ball and make the long throw to first base. The shortstop may play up to six steps back of the baseline if he has good range, a real strong arm, and a quick release when he throws. If either the arm or release is average, the shortstop should gain time to make plays by moving in a couple of steps toward the batter.

A smart shortstop can cheat and get a jump on where plays are likely to occur by paying attention to batters and the relationship to the pitcher's speed. If a pitcher has average speed or is slow, expect batters in the top half of the lineup to pull the ball. Move a couple of steps toward third for a right-handed pull hitter, toward second for a left-hander. For batters who swing late or if the pitcher is fast, cheat toward second base for right-handed batters and toward third for lefties.

Foul balls can give clues. Pull hitters pull fouls down the line. Fouls go straight back toward the backstop when the batter has the pitcher timed and will likely hit straightaway. It is hard to generalize all of this, but remember that the best hitters will bat in the upper half of the order, so look for weaker bats and late swingers in the lower half.

Double Play Depth

When there is a runner on first, fewer than two outs, and no other runners are in a position where the coach wants the infield to play in, move to double play depth. The position is a couple or three steps back of the baseline. Being slightly in can give the shortstop and second baseman time to try the double play. Double plays are not usually pulled off in the first level of youth baseball, but forcing the lead runner is a realistic expectation.

Playing In

In a game-saving situation with a runner on third and fewer than two outs, your coach may pull the infield in to get the runner trying to score. Move in to the baseline. If the bases are loaded, the play is at home to force the runner. If the runner at third isn't forced to go, field the ball and throw him out if he breaks toward the plate. If the runner doesn't break toward home, look him back, and throw the runner out at first. If the runner goes too far off third, he may present a pickoff opportunity at third.

Pop-Ups and Fly Balls

The shortstop will go out after fly balls to short left and center field and fair or foul flies behind third base. But an outfielder moving in to catch a fly ball has an easier play than an infielder moving out under the ball. The shortstop should be ready to be called off a fly by an outfielder in position to make the play. The shortstop calls "I've got it" and takes pop-ups and fly balls hit to his area. However, balls hit toward the pitcher, second, or third base require that the fielder in position to make the play calls for the ball.

Covering Bases

When there is a runner on first base, an attempted steal is always a possibility. Normally the shortstop will cover second when there is a lefty at the plate, and the second baseman will cover when the batter is right-handed. And some teams want the shortstop to always cover second on steals. The shortstop and second baseman must communicate and clarify which one will cover a steal. If the second baseman covers, the shortstop must back him up.

The shortstop covers third on a steal attempt when the third baseman plays in for a bunt. And the shortstop covers second base when the second baseman goes into the outfield for a relay throw.

Relay Plays

When a ball is hit to left or center field, the shortstop goes out toward the fielder to act as a cutoff and relay man. The shortstop sets up approximately one hundred feet from the outfielder and in line with the base where he anticipates the play. He should hold up his arms to provide the outfielder with a target for the throw. If there is only a runner on first when a single is hit, set up between the fielder and third base. If a runner is on second base and a single is hit, set up in line with home plate. Extra base hits or balls that get away from an outfielder generally require that the shortstop line up with a point between second and third. The infielder covering the base should call where to make the throw. When the shortstop takes a relay and the runners hold, the ball should be quickly carried back to the infield.

Making Tags

To make a tag, the shortstop straddles the bag, facing the incoming throw. He takes things in order: First, he makes sure to catch the ball. If it is a bad throw, he goes after it, then attempts to make the tag. When applying the tag, he holds the ball securely in the bare hand inside his glove. He makes a sure tag by bending down and placing the glove on the ground in front of the base where the runner must slide into it. One-handed tags, swipe tags, and high tags give runners good odds of being safe.

The Double Play

When a runner is on first or runners are on first and second bases with fewer than two outs, the shortstop moves to double play depth. When he fields a ground ball several feet from second base, the play is a toss to the second baseman who is covering the base. The toss should be toward the second baseman's chest, which makes it easy for him to handle. The first objective is to make sure to force the lead runner. If the second baseman makes the relay to complete a double play, it's a bonus. To develop the timing to make the force and relay to first takes a lot of practice on the part of both the shortstop and second baseman.

In the game situation above, when the ground ball is hit to the second baseman, sprint to second base. Take the throw from the second baseman with your foot firmly on the base to make the force play, then throw to first to complete the double play.

As stated before, most short-to-second-to-first double play attempts at the youth league level result in a force at second. But this doesn't mean players shouldn't practice turning a double play.

Tag-set-throw

However, when a good shortstop fields a hard ground ball as he is moving toward second base, the odds are good that he can step on second and throw to first base to complete the double play.

Other Plays

A line drive to the shortstop with runners on base presents an opportunity for a double play. The shortstop must always be aware of the position of the runners and alert teammates on where a play can be made. Again the fielder must make sure of the catch then make a throw to double off any runner who has wandered off base. If a runner on second has moved toward third when the ball was contacted, the shortstop may get an unassisted double play by tagging the runner.

When there are runners on first and second, a ground ball to the shortstop may present an opportunity to force the lead runner at third base. Generally, if the ball is hit toward the normal straightaway shortstop position and crosses the baseline in front of the runner, the shortstop can usually throw to third in time to force the runner. For this to work, the ball must be fielded cleanly. The other option is to take the force at second. Either play is good because it gets an out and takes a runner out of scoring position.

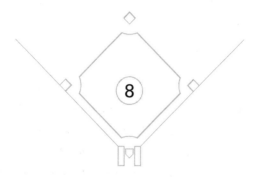

PLAYING THIRD BASE

Things happen quickly around third base, which is called "the hot corner" because good right-handed pull hitters hit the ball hard toward third base. Playing third base is not for the faint of heart. If you are afraid of the ball or turn your head on hard-hit grounders, you probably should not play third base.

CHARACTERISTICS OF A GOOD THIRD BASEMAN

A third baseman must consistently make long, accurate throws. For that reason, the third baseman must have a strong arm. Good third basemen do not need to be fast, because they usually do not need to move very far to make fielding plays. However, they need to have quick feet and hands to get to and field the ball. They need to be able to make strong, accurate snap throws. A youth league third baseman needs to be one of the best fielders on the team and be willing to get in front of hard-hit ground balls.

POSITIONING

Positioning for third base is very similar to positioning at first base, but at third base your basic fielding position should be two steps to the infield side of the base and even with the base.

In youth league games, most bunts go down the third baseline. You must be ready for bunts when the situation is right, and your coach should signal when to play in. In sacrifice bunt situations, you should play two steps in front of the base.

When you think a player is going to try to bunt for a base hit, you should play one step in front of the base. You can even get closer on left-handed hitters. However, if the hitter does not show a sign of bunting on the first two pitches, move back.

Have respect for the number three through six hitters in the lineup. You should play deep (a step or two behind the base and toward the baseline) for right-handed hitters and one step behind the base and two steps to your left for left-handed batters. Play deepest for the number three, four, and five hitters.

COMMON FIELDING PLAYS

Routine plays at third base are made the same way as at any other infield position. Certain plays that happen differently or more often at third base are discussed below.

The Hot Shot

Because most youth league hitters are right-handed, there is a good chance that some balls are going to be hit hard toward third base in every game. You probably will not have time to move to a hot shot. Making this play is simply a matter of quick reactions. Set yourself in the ready position (see chapter 1). If the ball is hit right at you, bend your knees and get your hands in position. Let the ball come to you. You will have plenty of time to throw. You might have to make a quick backhand or forehand "stab" for the ball with your glove hand. React as quickly as you can.

The Bunt or Weak Ground Ball

Third basemen have the major responsibility for balls bunted or softly tapped toward the third baseline. The weak ground ball (sometime called "a full swinging bunt") can actually be a harder play to make than the bunt, because you might not be expecting it. Always be ready for a weakly hit ground ball. On either a well-placed bunt or a weak ground ball, your first choice should usually be to get the out at first base because you will have more time to throw out the hitter than any other runner.

Some balls may slowly roll inside or on the foul line. You will have to decide whether to field the ball and make a throw or let the ball go into foul territory. Your first choice is to make the play if you can. You always want outs. If you let it go, touch the ball as soon as it crosses the foul line. When you touch the ball in foul territory, it officially becomes a foul ball. If the ball goes foul, hits a pebble, and then rolls back into fair territory without you touching it in foul territory, it will be a fair ball. The hitter will likely reach first base, and other runners will advance.

Ground Balls to Your Right or Left

The third baseman does not have much ground to cover to the right. You will usually have to backhand the ball. Always make the play to your right even if you think the ball might be a foul. Don't take a chance on the ball becoming a double down the line.

You should take charge on any ball hit to your left and field any ball you can get to that is hit to your left. You should move to your left in front of the shortstop because the play can be made faster and easier if you take it.

The High Hop

The third baseman seems to get more high (usually one-bounce) hops than any other infielder. Do not rush this play. Let the ball come to you. Be in a good throwing position when you catch the ball. You will have to put a little extra power into the throw.

Foul Ball Pop-Ups

Third basemen have special responsibilities for pop-ups in foul territory. Take charge on balls that you are sure you can catch. It is easier for you than the catcher to catch a ball that is popped up halfway between home plate and third base. Make the play if you can.

On balls that are popped straight over your head and are ten to twenty feet behind you, the play is easiest for the shortstop.

The shortstop also has the major responsibility for foul balls hit between third base and the left field corner. On both of these plays, you should turn, keep your eyes on the ball, and be ready to make the play until the shortstop calls the ball.

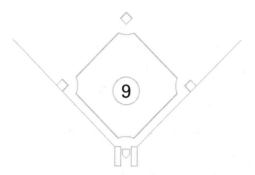

THE CATCHER

The catcher is the only defensive player who can see the entire field of play and has one of the most vital positions on a strong defensive team. The catcher has many jobs and must be a smart student of the game to excel at the position. He also must be willing to get down and get dirty. Catchers never want for action; they are involved in every play and must always know the game situation and how to react. And catching isn't the job for the faint of heart. He must be tough and remain calm no matter how tense the situation becomes.

CHARACTERISTICS OF A GOOD CATCHER

First, the catcher must handle the pitcher. The catcher calls each pitch and the location of the pitch by where he holds the target.

He must know the principles of hitting in order to help the pitcher work batters by spotting and pitching to batters' weaknesses. He must also know the pitcher well in order to give advice to help him get back on track when he is having control problems. If the pitcher shows signs of stress or tension, the catcher knows to call time-out and go to the mound to help calm him down. There's more on this at the end of this chapter.

The catcher must be a good, reliable receiver of pitches. The goal is to allow no passed balls. As a fielder he must catch pop-ups, field bunts, call defensive plays, cover the plate, back up some plays at first base, and pick off and throw out runners attempting to steal bases.

Physically a catcher should have a strong, accurate throwing arm, quick hands, and a durable body. The catcher should take on a leadership role on the field and set a good example for teammates by hustling at all times. Good catchers are aggressive and almost fearless. They accept the fact that they will occasionally be hit by foul tips, yet they never blink or flinch when a batter swings at a pitch.

EQUIPMENT

Be confident that your equipment will protect most of your body from foul tips, providing that the shin guards, chest protector, and mask properly fit your body. Make adjustments as needed. You will be using team gear, so make sure the chest protector covers your upper chest and neck area. The helmet should fit comfortably on your head, the mask must protect your face, and there must also be a throat protector in place. The shin guards should fit snugly and cover your knees and insteps. Always put on a shin guard with the buckles on the outside of your leg so they won't tangle and trip you.

At first, the equipment may feel awkward. To help get accustomed to it wear the equipment at all times when you're warming up pitchers or during infield drills. This will help you get used to catching, moving, and throwing while wearing full gear.

At first, you will also likely be using the team's catcher's mitt. But if you are serious about being a catcher, get your own mitt as soon as you can. Make sure the mitt fits your hand and is comfortable as you receive pitches. When a glove is used or broken in, the fingers will hinge toward the thumb as you catch the ball in the pocket.

Using a new catcher's mitt is like trying to catch a ball on a board until it is broken in. Most new mitts are stiff with a hard pocket, making the ball pop out of the glove as soon as it hits the pocket. To soften the leather of a new mitt, use some glove oil. Place a ball in the pocket and bind the mitt tightly around the ball overnight with rope or rubber binders. Work the hinge back and forth toward the thumb with your hands to loosen it. While these things help with the break-in process, nothing beats catching a lot of pitches until the new mitt loosens up.

CATCHER RESPONSIBILITIES

Becoming a good catcher takes work, lots of it. It is not easy to develop the skills and mind-set necessary to be a good catcher. The player must accept a large share of the responsibility for a team's defensive effectiveness. This position is only for those who really want to play it.

Giving the Signal

The catcher uses signals to suggest each pitch. In the first league games the signals will be simple. Pitches at the youth level will likely be the fastball, changeup, and pitchout. Later, in older levels of play the pitch assortment can include several other pitches

Give signal

including curveballs, sliders, knuckleballs, and many others. But at every level, communication between catcher and pitcher on each pitch is essential. The catcher also signals the location where he wants the pitch.

To give the signal, squat down in position behind home plate, just out of range of the batter's swing. You are bent only at the knees and waist. Your feet should be from ten to twelve inches apart, and your knees will be pointed slightly outward. Your back is straight. Rest your left forearm on your left knee and drop your mitt, palm inward, slightly in front of your left knee. (The glove should block any attempt of a third base coach from stealing the signal.)

Place your right hand close to your crotch next to your right thigh and give the signal with your fingers and hand. Signal systems vary, but in the younger youth leagues, one would normally be a fastball, two a curveball (if the pitcher is allowed to throw one), three a changeup, and a fist for a pitchout. (Pitchouts will usually be called by a coach from the dugout in steal situations.) Following the number signal, the catcher can also signal where he wants the pitch by moving his hand right or left to indicate he wants an inside or outside pitch.

If the signals are given properly, neither base coach can steal them. However, when a runner is on second, most teams use an alternate set of signs with many variations. One way is to give two or three sets of signals with the second one being the real signal.

Receiving

After giving the signal, raise up, then go to a receiving position. Your feet should be spread slightly wider than your shoulders with your toes pointing slightly outward. Your heels should be on the ground, but your weight will be slightly forward on the balls of your feet. Your left foot should be slightly forward of your right foot. You should be close to the batter but not so close that you interfere with the swing. In this position you are ready to shuffle to throw to a base, sprint out to field a bunt, or drop to block a low pitch.

Bend at the waist and knees to get your body low in the strike zone. With your arms bent at a ninety-degree angle, hold your glove forward and open toward the pitcher with the fingers up to

Target

give a target. (In almost all cases you will want to give a low target at the knees.) The pitcher's control can determine if you hold the target down the middle of the plate or on a corner, but this will be covered in a later section on working batters.

Hold the glove fingers up when giving the target, and hold the target still until the pitcher releases the pitch. Focus on the ball and watch it all the way to your mitt. Catch pitches above your waist with the fingers up. Pitches below the waist are to be caught with the fingers down. Develop "soft" hands as you catch. Your glove hand gives a little as the ball hits the glove, and your bare hand covers the ball and grasps it to throw immediately after it hits the mitt.

Old-time catchers were known by their many often broken fingers. One way to protect your bare hand is to make a semi-fist with

Make a fist

Behind glove

the fingers clenched, partially closed, and the thumb bent under the index finger. The other way is to hold the bare hand behind the thumb of the catcher's mitt. You want to catch pitches with both hands, quickly get a grip on the ball, and be ready to throw.

Blocking Bad Pitches

Keep your body square, facing toward the ball, and drop to both knees with your glove in front of the ball to block low pitches. You may be able to scoop or pick a low pitch cleanly with your glove, but dropping down ensures that you'll keep the ball from rolling to

Drop to block a low pitch

the backstop. At the least, if you don't handle a low pitch cleanly, you want to keep it out in front of your position where you can pick it up and make a play if needed.

A pitch that bounces alongside or in front of the plate will bounce high. To block a high bouncer, keep your body square in front of the ball and stop it with your body.

Throwing

First, don't work your pitcher. When you are returning the ball to the pitcher, make a good waist-high, medium-speed throw. Your pitcher needs all of his energy to do his job, don't make him waste effort chasing bad throws.

One of the big defensive contributions a catcher can make is to throw out runners attempting to steal bases. Once a catcher has nailed a few runners, word gets around the league and only the fastest runners will even try to steal. On the other hand, if a catcher can't make the throws, this can allow other teams' runners a free pass to a scoring position a couple of pitches after they reach first base.

There are three attributes a catcher needs to effectively cut down would-be base thieves. Arm strength and accuracy are both important, and the third attribute is a quick release. An accurate, quick release can, to some extent, make up for a lack of arm strength. To put it another way, a strong arm seldom makes up for a slow release. The quickness and efficiency of your footwork goes a long way in developing a quick release. You must learn to get into a throwing position quickly while remaining balanced. The other part is fast hands. Put on full gear and practice taking pitches and making good, quick throws to the bases until the movement becomes almost automatic.

At your young age, your strongest, most accurate throwing motion will be overhand or three-quarter overhand. Use the method that gives you the best accuracy. When you make a throw, pick the ball out of your mitt and raise your hand back into the throwing position. Some catchers reach back to throw harder, others raise the hand near the ear to make a snap throw.

As you receive the ball, your footwork should have you almost in a position to make the throw. In your receiving position, your left foot is slightly in advance of your right foot. Let's say a runner is trying to steal second base with the pitch. If the pitch is inside or down the middle across the plate, shuffle-step your weight onto your right foot as you receive the ball. Grip the ball, bringing your arm and hand to the throwing position as you step toward second with your left foot and make the throw to the base.

Receive the pitch

Shuffle-step to plant right foot

Stride toward target and cock arm to throw

Release

If the pitch is outside to a right-handed batter or inside to a lefty, you may need to make the shuffle step to the right with your right foot as you receive the ball. Then you step toward the base with your left foot to make the throw. This may also be the foot-work you use on a throw to third base when the pitch is inside to a right-handed batter.

Steal Plays

When there is only a runner on first base who tries to steal second, the play is simple: throw him out. If runners on first and second try a double steal, again the play is simple: take the runner going toward third. It gets a little more complicated with runners on first and third bases, and teams have many different defensive setups for this situation. The following are some options.

If there are two outs, and you are confident in your ability to get a runner at second, take him to end the inning. With fewer than two outs, you risk giving up a run by going after the runner at second. If the runner drifts off third base, you may try to pick him off. Another option is to make a quick throw back to the pitcher who tries to throw out either runner.

A play that takes a lot of coordination goes like this: Make a quick throw short of second base. An aggressive runner at third may break toward the plate. The shortstop cuts in front of second, takes the throw, and makes the play on the runner trying to score. For any of these plays you must be ready to cover the plate and make a tag.

Fielding Pop-Ups

Any fielder moving in on a fly ball has a better angle to make a catch than a fielder moving out under the ball. So, the first and third basemen should take any pop-ups hit between their position and home plate.

When a pop-up goes up, immediately take off your mask and helmet and hold it in your right hand. Find the ball in the air and toss the mask and helmet away from the area where the ball will come down. Pop-ups in the area of the plate and in foul territory toward the backstop are your responsibility. Move toward the ball as it descends. Catch it with your glove and bare hand, palms up, close to your chest.

Short pop-ups go up and come down straight toward the ground. High pop-ups react differently when they descend because the bat imparts a spin to the ball on contact. This spin causes a high pop-up to descend with what is called "infield drift." In effect, the ball goes up, reaches the apex in flight, then curves toward the infield as it falls toward the ground. Being aware of infield drift, you should circle to the left of a high pop-up to your right and circle to the right of a pop-up to your left. Move toward the ball with your back toward the infield. As you move toward the ball to catch it, the drift will move the ball toward you.

Fielding Bunts

In your receiving position, your right foot is slightly farther back than your left foot. You are balanced on the balls of your feet, which can give you a fast start to sprint out to field a bunt. As soon as the batter bunts, flip your mask and helmet off the back of your head, and run out from under it.

Bare hand pickup when bunt has stopped

A bunt that carries out up to four or five steps from the plate will be your play. Call off other fielders ("I've got it") as you approach the ball. You will field bunts from the left of the ball. For example, if the bunt is down the third baseline and the play is

Circle and scoop up rolling bunt

at first, circle to the left of the ball. Circle less for the play at first when the bunt is toward the pitcher, and even less when the bunt goes down the first baseline. For plays to any base, if your footwork is correct when you field the bunt, a line drawn across your toes will be pointing toward the base where you make the play. If the ball has stopped rolling, pick it up with your bare hand, step toward the base, keeping balanced, and make the throw. If the bunt is rolling, block in front of it with your mitt, scoop it into your hand, set your feet, and make the throw.

Hard bunts out of the catcher's range will be fielded either by the pitcher, first baseman, or third baseman. Because the fielder's back is to any base runners, the catcher calls the number of the base to make the play. In most cases the sure play is at first. But there will be situations when your team can put out a lead runner. For example, a hard bunt goes directly to the pitcher, and it is obvious that there is time to force a runner advancing toward second. The catcher calls "go two." The pitcher then turns and throws out the lead runner.

Covering Home Plate

In a perfect world all throws to home plate would be easy to handle. But many throws will be to one side of the plate or the other, or they will bounce in the dirt. When there is a play at the plate, the chips are down, a runner is trying to score. You must handle the throw. Your first priority is to go after the ball and try to field it cleanly. It is best if you don't go out to meet the ball or back up on a bouncer to make the catch. Move to your left or right as needed to catch the ball, then set up to make the tag. Drop down and block a throw in the dirt. If you don't pick it cleanly, at least you can block it to keep the ball in front of you.

Making Tags

Once you have received the throw, set up to make the tag at the plate. Place your left foot on the third base side of the plate and drop to your right knee on the right side of the plate. Grasp the ball tightly in your hand in the pocket of your mitt and hold it in front of the third base corner of the plate. You will be tagging the

Tag in front of plate

Recieve throw for force play

runner as he slides with the back of the mitt. The throw may be up the third baseline, or you may get the throw in time to go up the line and tag him as he is running. To tag a runner, again grasp the ball tightly in your mitt with both hands and tag him on the side with the mitt.

Force Plays

When there is a force play at home, stand behind the plate and face the player making the throw. For a throw over the plate, step on the plate with your right foot and step forward in front of the plate with your left foot. Keep your right foot on the plate until you catch the ball. If the throw is to either side of the plate, step toward the throw and drag the opposite foot across the plate to complete the force.

There are two things to remember when covering home plate. First, you can't block the plate without possession of the ball. And second, at the completion of any tag or force play, come up from the play ready to make a throw to a base. You may be able to complete a double play or catch a runner trying to advance.

Pickoff Plays

Watch base runners after you receive pitches. Although in the youngest youth leagues runners can't lead off bases, some runners try to bluff a steal with the pitch or just wander off base. Don't make a bunch of bluff throws. Have a pickoff signal with your first and third basemen. You don't need to call for a pitchout. Give the signal for the infielder to cover the bag and pick the runner off after the next pitch. Make your throw low on the infield side of the base where it is easy for the infielder to catch and make the tag.

Working with Your Pitcher

The catcher and the pitcher make up the battery. How well you work together will have a lot to do with the outcome of any game because the two of you are the core of the team's defense. From control drills, practice, warm-ups, and game experience, you should know a lot about your pitcher. Questions you should be able to answer are: Does he have good control? Can he spot pitches in the strike zone? What are his best pitches? What batters or situations cause him the most trouble? What is his relative pitch speed, and can he blow a fastball past most batters? Is he usually calm or nervous and excitable? How does he deal with pressure? Knowing these things can help you work effectively with him to get batters out.

You can control the pace of the game to suit how the pitcher wants to work. If he's a fast worker, return the ball to him quickly. If he wants some time between pitches, you can be slower about giving him the ball without noticeably delaying the game.

When things get tough, encourage your pitcher to keep him on a positive course. Review things with him that go right and those that go wrong. Try to learn together from both types of experiences. Calm him down if he starts to tighten up. You need to be his partner and strongest supporter.

Working Batters

Fooling batters and getting them out is the most fun you and your pitcher can have in a game. This is where working together as a team pays big dividends. You are close to the batters where you can observe things that will help your pitcher. You call for pitches and a location for the pitch by where you hold your target. You must think with your pitcher and have a purpose for each pitch you call.

You must have your head in the game at all times. You both must know the game situation and where you are in the other team's batting order. Check with your team's scorer to see what batters did the last time they went to the plate. You will work more carefully with the stronger batters in the top half of the order than the weaker hitters at the bottom. Always try to help your pitcher get ahead of batters in the count. When you're behind in the count, just have him throw strikes. There's no defense for a base on balls.

The following are some things to look for when batters are at the plate and how to take advantage of them, including suggestions for spotting pitches. But pitchers don't always have great control. The best pitch will always be a strike.

Late swinger—The ball is in your glove before the batter swings, or his best effort is a weak foul ball to the opposite field. Give this batter a steady diet of good fastballs. This batter will likely be in the bottom part of the order. Never change up on a late swinger, it's the only pitch slow enough for him to hit.

Pull hitter—This is a right-handed batter who strides down the third baseline or a lefty who strides down the first baseline. This batter needs an inside pitch, hold the target on the outside corner. An outside pitch is very hard to pull; low and outside is even harder.

Scared batter—This batter sets up so far away from the plate that he can barely reach a pitch down the middle. Strike him out with outside pitches.

Plate crowder—This batter will try to hang ten over the inside corners of the plate and is trying to take the plate away from your pitcher. He wants the pitcher to pitch away, probably trying to draw a base on balls. Hold your target inside. The crowder will only be able to hit the ball on the handle.

Beggar—The pitch is perfect, right down the middle, and the batter shows no inclination to swing. This batter is likely hoping to beg a walk. Hold your target down the middle; make him hit his way on base.

Good hitter—The batter fouls a fastball straight back to the backstop. This hitter has your pitcher timed. Mess with his timing by mixing changeups with fastballs.

OTHER CATCHER DUTIES

There will be wild pitches and hopefully few passed balls that you must hustle to retrieve and make any plays the situation warrants.

With no runners on base, you hustle to back up throws to first base when there is a ground ball play in the infield.

With no runners on base, you cover first base when the first baseman goes after a fly ball.

FINALLY

Now that you've read and studied all of the catcher's duties, skills, and responsibilities, you must now understand why learning to be a catcher is only for those who really want to play the position.

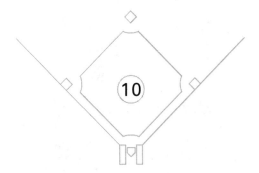

THE PITCHER'S
ROLE IN DEFENSE

The moment you release a pitch and follow through, you become a fifth infielder. In your follow-through position, you are facing the plate, head up, feet square with your weight on the balls of your feet. This is also the ready position of the other infielders. Pitching isn't all about balls and strikes. You have opportunities in every game to get putouts or make assists if you can field your position well. And, if your fielding is deficient, you can make trouble for your team by allowing batters to reach base and runners to advance. Each runner you retire is one less you'll need to face at the plate.

Follow-through position

Pitchers should always be included in infield practice work-ups. The coordination in the infield to properly execute plays in different game situations takes timing that can best be learned by repetition in practice, practice, and more practice.

FIELDING PLAYS

Before each pitch, think about the situation and where you will make the play if you field the ball. Your reaction to make the correct play should be automatic.

Comeback Hits

You will have balls hit right back at you. Pitchers seem to get more than a few during a game when they are fooling the batters.

When there are no runners on base, a hard comeback hit is an easy play for a pitcher. There is plenty of time to catch the ball, step toward first base, and throw the runner out.

A hard comebacker can present a good opportunity to kill the other team's rally. In regulation Little League play the bases are only sixty feet apart, but the runners can't lead off base. With a runner on first base, after fielding a hard comeback hit, you can usually force the runner going to second. If there are runners on first and second, you may get the runner going to third. And with the bases loaded the play is the force at home.

If for any reason (such as bobbling the ball, stumbling, or being off balance after making a tough play) you feel you can't get the lead runner in these situations, your option is to take the out at first. Getting a lead runner is important, and when the catcher or infielder makes a throw to complete a double play, it's a bonus. But at a minimum you must get an out.

If there is no runner at first base, but there are runners on second or third, you don't have a force play. Catch the ball and look the runners back to the base. If one tries to advance, throw him out. If a runner starts to advance then stops between bases, run right at him. Throw him out or make a throw to trap him in a rundown when he breaks for a base. If the runners hold, your option is to turn and take the out at first.

A line drive or looping fly ball back to the mound presents an opportunity to double off any runners who leave a base when the ball is contacted. You know where these runners are, turn ready to step and throw as soon as you catch the ball.

Slow Rollers

If you pay attention to the game situation, you know where to make plays on a hard-hit comebacker. However, you may need help on bunts and slow-rolling ground balls. The catcher is in the best position to call the base to make the play. With no runners on base, the obvious play is to first. With a runner on first or runners on first and second, you may have time to make a throw to force a lead runner. When you field the ball, the catcher should call "go one" for a play at first or "go two" for a play at second, and so on. However, on most slow rollers, your only play is at first.

Fielding Bunts

Batters can bunt almost any pitch. A pitcher who can't field bunts and throw out runners can be bunted out of the park. But the pitcher isn't the only infielder who will handle bunts. Depending on how the coach sets up the bunt defense, the pitcher may only field bunts in a certain area. Teams test bunt defenses, and batter after batter may bunt until the team proves it can make the play. Make sure you can do your part by practicing long and hard at getting to bunts, fielding them, and making good throws to each base.

When a bunt is rolling, block in front of it with your glove, scoop it into your bare hand, grip it, set your back foot, and make the throw. Pick up a bunt that has stopped with your bare hand and make the play. If a bunt along a baseline looks like it will roll into foul territory, let it roll and touch it with your glove or bare hand as soon as it crosses the foul line.

Usually, your only play on a bunt is to first base, but a hard bunt back to you may allow you to cut down a lead runner. Listen to your catcher: he should call the play. A bunt that is popped up may allow you to double a runner off base.

Depending on your coach's bunt defense, the first and third basemen may be charging in on all bunts. It's possible that you, the catcher, the first baseman, or the third baseman will field a bunt. Whoever will play it must quickly call off the other players.

Making the Throws

Some of the throws you make after fielding the ball are simple. Examples of these plays are the throw to first when you get a hard comeback or to home for a force when the bases are loaded. When you throw to second to force a runner, the middle infielder may not be at the base. In this case your throw should be between the fielder and the base. When you field a bunt, the throw to first should be on the infield side of the base to avoid striking the runner.

Covering the Bases

When a ground ball is hit out of your reach toward the first base side of the infield, continue toward first to cover it. If the first baseman is at the base, or he has fielded the ball and will make the play unassisted, he should call you off the play. When the first baseman cannot make the play, you must cover first. Sprint to a point along the first baseline ten or fifteen feet short of first base. Turn and run along and inside the baseline (in fair territory) toward the base to avoid colliding with the runner. In this position you are almost facing the throw. Take the throw and step on the infield side of the bag to get the out.

Covering first base

You must really hustle to make this play at first base. The play requires good timing with the infielder making the throw to you. In many cases you will take the toss or throw while you are moving toward the base. With hard practice you can get it right.

If the shortstop and second baseman go out into center field for a fly ball, you must cover second. And if the third baseman and shortstop go after a fly ball to left field, you must cover third base.

You must cover home plate when there is a runner in scoring position and the catcher leaves his position to field a pop-up or a pitch gets past the catcher. Sprint toward home the instant you see a pitch get by the catcher. Straddle the plate, facing the catcher, keeping your foot out of the baseline. Take the throw and hold the ball in both hands in front of the third base side of the plate to tag the runner. Do not attempt to block the plate. A collision can cause a serious injury.

Backing Up Bases

With runners on base or when there is an extra-base hit, you must back up plays at third base and home plate. Anticipate where the play will be and position yourself from twenty to thirty feet behind the fielder making the play. This should give you enough space to back up the play if the ball gets loose.

The general guidelines are if there is a runner on first and the batter gets a base hit, you would back up third base. If it is an extra-base hit, back up home plate. If there is a runner on second base and the batter gets a hit, back up home plate. With a runner at third base and the batter hitting a sacrifice fly, you should back up home. If you're not sure which base to back up, go to a point halfway between home and third base and move to the proper position as the play develops.

THE PITCHER'S ADVANTAGE

It is rare on a Little League–age team for a pitcher to specialize in pitching only. Pitchers are usually the better athletes on a team, meaning that they play another position when they aren't on the mound. This is great for player development because a player may hold many different positions during a career. For the present, the experience gained at another position gives pitchers an edge in fielding. Fielding plays and the footwork to make good throws should be easy for a pitcher playing another position. The focus must be on the game situations and where to make the proper play.

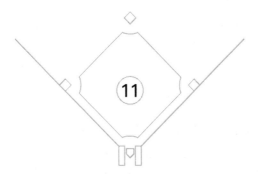

GAME-WINNING DEFENSE

As stated before, a strong defensive team will be in most ball games because good defense keeps the score close, giving the team a chance to win. In years of coaching and umpiring, we have witnessed as many or more ball games being lost by bad defense and unearned runs than games won by an overpowering offense. A good defense must make plays to overcome the pressure an offensive team can exert by aggressive hitting, bunting, and attempting to steal bases. A winning defense, which we describe in this chapter, doesn't crack under pressure.

FUNDAMENTALLY SOUND

First and foremost a winning defense is fundamentally sound at all positions. Fielders move to the ball aggressively and with a purpose. They field throws, ground balls, and fly balls cleanly with soft hands. Their footwork is sure, and they make crisp, accurate throws. The mechanics of catching, fielding, throwing, and making sure tags are the foundation of good defensive play and can only be developed and improved through practice, practice, and more practice.

STRONG UP THE MIDDLE

It's an old baseball truism that a good defense must be "strong up the middle." Of course, strong pitching is the cornerstone of a defense, but this isn't about pitching. The pitcher becomes an infielder the instant he releases a pitch and must be able to field his position well. The other positions in a defense that is strong up the middle are catcher, shortstop, second baseman, and center fielder. Statistically most of the plays will be made by fielders in these positions, and coaches usually fill these field positions with players they expect to make plays and lead the defense. This does not diminish or put down the importance of the other positions in the field. All defensive positions are important, and each has a role to play. For example, some young players feel they are being punished when they are positioned in right field, but if the team has a fast pitcher, the right fielder will likely get a lot of balls hit toward his position from right-handed batters because of the pitch speed and late swings.

LOOSE AND READY

All players on a winning defense are prepared to go after the ball to make a play as each pitch is delivered. Fielders' bodies are in a ready position, their eyes are focused on the ball, but the fielders are not rooted at their position. If you look carefully, each player's feet are moving slightly in little shuffle steps as the pitch approaches the batter. These small steps do not commit a player to a specific direction or affect his balance, but they do have the fielder moving, ready to get a quick start as he goes to field a batted ball.

KNOW THE PLAY

Players at all positions stay aware of the game situation. They listen to their coaches and call out where to make the next play. They are aware of when to anticipate a bunt, steal, or hit-and-run play by the offense. Each player knows his job on each play and when to cover a base or when to back up the play. Relays from the outfield go to a cutoff man, and the throw to the proper base is called by another player. Players communicate with their teammates so that when a player calls for a fly ball or pop-up, other teammates respect the call and back off to let him make the catch.

A winning defense knows that getting lead runners out is important. And with a runner on second or third with fewer than two outs, the infielders know how to look the runner back and then take the out at first. A winning defense concedes very little. With runners on first and third and fewer than two outs, there will be a play if the runner at first tries to steal second. But, when playing with a big lead, the team may allow a runner on third base to score on a ground ball, taking the out at first base.

Runners who stray off base will be in danger of a pickoff throw. And, when a runner is caught in a rundown, infielders chase him back toward the preceding base. If they don't get the out, the runner doesn't advance.

CONFIDENCE AND TRUST

Finally, players on a winning defense all know their jobs on each play. They have confidence in each other's ability to make plays, they work together as a unit, and they communicate well and consistently perform well. The pitcher knows he can throw strikes and trust his defense to make plays. To develop a good team defense requires a coach's emphasis and intense practice. Practicing defense and learning to field and throw well are not the most exciting facets of playing baseball, but they are vital elements in a successful, winning baseball team.

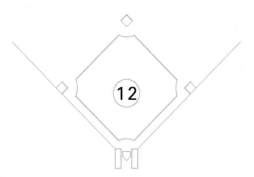

FINAL THOUGHTS

Throughout this book, we have talked about the skills and techniques involved in effective defensive play. Beyond making plays to get batters and runners out, there is a psychological side to defense, and this relates to how players may react when the defense on their team isn't sound. When a team is not confident on defense, doubt creeps in, leading to breakdowns that can cause team losses. In fact, weak defensive teams more often than not actually beat themselves. It can start with an error on a simple play, and the thought of "here we go again" creeps in.

So what can individual players do? Simply put, each player must do his job. It starts with the fundamentals of fielding and throwing. These basic skills must be a given in order for a fielder to play any position well. To develop these skills takes hours of practice at throwing and catching. In time, catching a ball and making a good throw should be automatic. Keeping your head in the game, knowing the situation and where to make the plays, and using the basic fielding fundamentals will result in good defensive execution. When all position players on a team have these elements down pat, a team will have a strong defense. Preventing the other team from scoring is a major key to team success. Again, it requires hard work, knowledge of the game, and focus for a team to reach this point.

As a young player, you should try to learn to play as many different positions as possible. Your sound fielding and throwing fundamentals will apply to each one. Your versatility and defensive ability may make the difference in your being drafted, making ball teams, or being selected on all-star teams. As you progress beyond the youth baseball level, experience at playing different positions again can be valuable. Your baseball career is just beginning now. Working hard at developing your defensive skills can put you on the path to becoming a complete baseball player.

ABOUT THE AUTHORS

Don Oster is a longtime baseball player and coach who, as his friends claim, joined the dark side when he started umpiring. He is now an Indiana high school baseball and softball umpire. He managed a Little League World Series baseball team from Minnesota in 1985, a state champion Babe Ruth league team in 1986, and was pitching coach on four Babe Ruth World Series teams. He is the author of *Largemouth Bass* and coauthor of *A Guide for Young Pitchers*; *A Guide for Young Batters and Baserunners*; *A Guide for Young Softball Pitchers*; *A Young Softball Player's Guide to Hitting, Bunting, and Baserunning*; *Hunting Today's Whitetail*; and *Pronghorn Hunting*. He lives in southern Indiana.

Bill McMillan has twenty years' experience as a manager and pitching coach at the youth level. His teams have won nine league championships and a Minnesota State Little League title. He is coauthor of *A Guide for Young Pitchers* and *A Guide for Young Batters and Baserunners*. He has served as both a public school teacher and a university professor. Bill holds a PhD in educational psychology and has worked extensively at both state and national levels on various educational programs.